T0381302

JUST A THOUGHT

Richard Byrd

AuthorHouse™
1663 Liberty Drive
Bloomington, IN 47403
www.authorhouse.com
Phone: 1 (800) 839-8640

Published by AuthorHouse 08/03/2018

ISBN: 978-1-5462-5228-3 (sc)
ISBN: 978-1-5462-5229-0 (e)

Library of Congress Control Number: 2018908674

Print information available on the last page.

Any people depicted in stock imagery provided by Getty Images are models, and such images are being used for illustrative purposes only. Certain stock imagery © Getty Images.

This book is printed on acid-free paper.

Just a Thought

Richard Byrd

Existence is only
a reflection of life
in the flesh...
just a thought

Self justification never provided
anything to a crowd...
just a thought

Inventory of ourselves
is always necessary
when we are being judgemental
of someone else...
just a thought

Hope is a tremendous obstacle
to someone who looks
forward to failure...
just a thought

Hope is a tremendous goal
to reach for a hopeless mind,
our biggest defects
are centered in the way we think...
just a thought

Things are taken
without your permission
when you take them for granted...
just a thought

Moving beyond your counterparts
or friends, to outgrow
the usual environments,
is to mature...
just a thought

You will be noticed,
if you stop trying
so hard to be seen...
just a thought

Resentment is a spiritual disease,
it allows you to take
on someone else's issues
without your permission...
just a thought

Excuses are tools of denial,
used to build monuments of failure and
those who specializes in them seldom
amount to any kind of status
or responsibility...
just a thought

Imagination is what dreams are made of,
it's a basis to explore an unknown universe,
to help enhance our spiritual awareness to
find some knowledge that normally
would be out of reach...
just a thought

When the story becomes a lie,
then who's telling it...
just a thought

Rebirth and renewal of the mind
will always open up new
horizons to explore...
just a thought

The personal life, that last life
didn't have social situations that were
worth while to continue and nobody
could depend on us, so dramatically
we changed our way of thinking,
to improve the atmosphere, by giving back
what has been freely given to us
and then we could live life
on life's terms once more...
just a thought.

Money and friends are a lot alike,
easy to get but hard to keep...
just a thought

In any relationship we must know that
love, comfort and support
will last longer than
any materialistic idea...
just a thought

Some people think
that a sexual relationship
is a part of growing up,
but to their surprise,
they realize to late,
that immorality isn't a way
to find immortality...
just a thought

Comments are just opinions
without much thought behind them...
just a thought

Your past didn't open the gates of Heaven
to let you in,
it opened the gates of Hades
to let you out...
just a thought

Many people believe in nothing
but nothing from nothing
leaves nothing...
just a thought

Eventhough you are a religious person,
it doesn't mean that
you are spiritually connected...
just a thought

Temptation is the worm
that the apple keeps hidden...
just a thought

Sometimes people get what they want
instead of what they need
and at the end of the day,
they lose whatever they had...
J.A.TH.

We are designed to move forward,
it is only optional to look
or go backwards...
just a thought

It takes a system of checks and balances
to understand how aware we are
to be secure enough
in whatever life has to offer...
J.A.TH

Good judgment
becomes common sense
when you have a open mind...
just a thought

Pain can only hold you hostage
if you won't let it go...
just a thought

It's better to be poor with integrity
than to be rich with no friends...
just a thought

I've took my eyes off yesterday
and threw the keys away,
tomorrow has no fear for me
since I have today...
just a thought

The delusion is when your mind tells you
that the allusion is real,
as if to say that your girlfriend or boyfriend
is your husband or wife...
just a thought

A child learns discipline from the adults
but if the adults doesn't plant the seeds,
they receive no harvest...
just a thought

Some will panic in desperate times,
but desperation is only a false state of
mind, that has lost it's faith
for that moment when to be strong
wasn't entirely enough...
just a thought

Death is never final
for those who are
just passing on...
just a thought

Fantastic stories
can come from bad decision
and wrong turns...
just a thought

The awesomeness of one individual
can be immeasurable,
depending on whose
taking the measurements..
just a thought

Self-justification
never helped the accused...
just a thought

If I could turn back
the hands of time,
I would lose the reality
of my own experiences...
just a thought

We can never pay
for our own peace of mind
at the expense of someone else...
just a thought

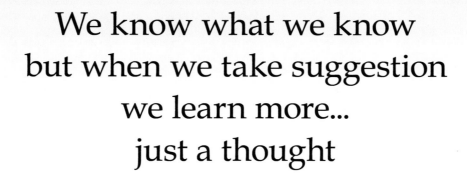

We know what we know
but when we take suggestion
we learn more...
just a thought

A fool is always right
in his or her own mind...
just a thought

To be warm-hearted, generous
and friendly towards others
is to be kind with whoever
comes our way...
just a thought

Nothing changes who you use to be,
accept who you are becoming today...
just a thought

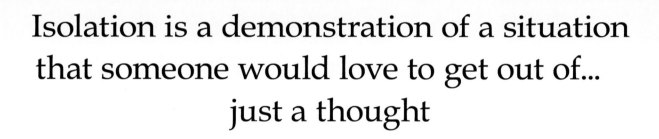

Isolation is a demonstration of a situation
that someone would love to get out of...
just a thought

Going out without any principles
is like going outside without a coat,
there's a possibility
that you may catch a cold...
J.A.TH

Somewhere between
nowhere and goodbye
is moving on...
just a thought

We may go many miles in a lifetime,
travel many roads in a day
and still end up right where
we are supposed to be...
J.A.TH.

Knowledge is what we know,
information is what we seek to know
and experience is the active
participation of them both...
J.A.TH.

Jealousy is a state of mind
in which trust is not included
and insecurities take control...
just a thought

GOD may take you places
that old friends may not be able to follow
when you find your purpose...
just a thought

Never push people away
just because you are going
through something,
all that does is leave you alone...
just a thought

Reconciliation is the peace
that comes with forgiveness...
just a thought

DEPENDENCY- The phenomenon
is like a imaginary image
that sometimes consist of a dependency, of
emotional imbalances that stimulates
the brain into a consumption,
of a false release, of a sensational
satisfaction and it's never enough...
J.A.TH.

Being single is a choice
that very few people
likes' to keep...
just a thought

A problem is just a issue
that haven't been faced
with a solution...
just a thought

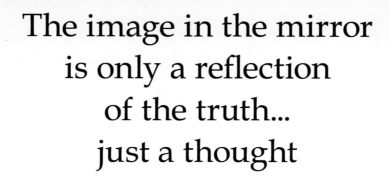

The image in the mirror
is only a reflection
of the truth...
just a thought

The clay pot can be broken now
and then just to be mended back
together again...
just a thought

If you knew your final destination
then you wouldn't be going
through your temporary situation...
just a thought

The best way to overcome
everyone else's problems
is to not make them your own...
just a thought

Seeking material possessions
is like looking for life
in all the wrong places,
you can't take it with you...
just a thought

When the time comes
it will never be about
how you died or from what
but how did you live...
just a thought

Just like a mountain
can not be moved by the storm,
you should not be moved
by what they say or think...
just a thought

A curious mind cannot be stopped
when it wants to know
why is this or that...
just a thought

Friends are never lost
when associated with
good memories...
just a thought

Nobody is born knowing that
hardships and mistakes
would be the pathway
to peace and stability...
just a thought

Today if you want a
brighter tomorrow
then do better than
you did yesterday...
just a thought

Living the dream
on plan B...
just a thought

Everything will go
from day to night
from life to death
from moments to memories
without your permission...
just a thought

The best thing about being human
is that there is a greater version
of yourself just waiting to be released...
just a thought

Physical feelings
will forget about the touch
once it has been released...
just a thought

Just a thought

Understanding and knowledge
are very different,
you can have knowledge of me
and no understanding of who I am...
just a thought

There's a beginning and a end,
everything else disappears
in-between...
just a thought

They get rich off
other people's
sufferings and call
it charity...
just a thought

Like the spokes on a wheel,
we all have a equal part
to play and a purpose...
just a thought

A bad day is just
another day to do a
little more readjusting...
just a thought

People pleasers will
never say what's on
their mind...
just a thought

If you think that you are a loser,
then you've already lost,
your only limits are the obstacles
in your mind or thinking...
J.A.TH.

Our primary focus
should never become
our secondary goals...
just a thought

All dignity is lost
when the fool
shows up...
just a thought

The greatest value
that no currency
could ever have is trust...
just a thought

The biggest hearts
are within the children,
humbleness is to love
as a child loves...
just a thought

Single is not a
choice or decision,
it's a cry for
companionship..
just a thought

Luck is only the illusion
of the chance that it may
or may not happen...
just a thought

Where you were
and where you are
will never end up
in the same place...
just a thought

Rejection will push
you away just like
broken promises...
just a thought

A wise person once said that
if you don't have any experience
on the matter then just listen,
you may just learn something...
JATH.

Mistakes will be made,
imperfection is the root
of being human...
just a thought

Discipline isn't just an opportunity
to symbolize with our
self improvement in life,
it's accompanied by counter questioning
and continuing with our
own self examination...
just a thought

Dead weight needs
to be left behind
even though it may
feel like you may
have just lost your
best friend...
just a thought

Specially and specifically designed,
fundamentally sound,
human with every(i) dotted
and every(t) crossed we are made,
no instrument or tool has ever been created
with such detail or functionality...
just a thought

We must remove the impurities
within the elements of our spirits
to process the changes
that we would want to take place
within our souls...
just a thought

Dead space in a
lifetime of experience,
is a lesson learned...
just a thought

Self assessment is
taking a deep look
into myself, at who I
was yesterday, who
I am today and who
I would like to be
tomorrow
JATH

See without hindrance,
to get rid of the mist
and haze that is
obstructing your
vision, look and
envision with love
and truth.
JATH

Be like a sponge
and soak in the joy
of living...
just a thought

Resentment is a
spiritual disease,
it allows you to take
on someone else's
issues without your
permission...
just a thought

People say,
let's just get along
but nobody is willing
to take the first step...
just a thought

You can sit back
and watch things happen
or you can get up
and help make them happen...
just a thought

Because they say, I love you,
it doesn't mean that they are
in love with you,
love and lust
are not the same...
just a thought

Don't just be a woman,
be the woman
that is in demand...
just a thought